THE SIX PASSIONS
OF THE RED-HOT LOVER

THE SIX PASSIONS OF THE RED-HOT LOVER

Find out which one is yours

Wendy Brown
Clinical Member, Ontario Society of Pyschotherapists

Copyright © 2016 by Wendy Brown

All rights reserved. No part of this publication may be reproduced, stored in a retrieval system, or transmitted, in any form or by any means, electronic, mechanical, photocopying, recording, or otherwise, without the prior written permission of the author.

For information about permission to reproduce sections of this book, email Wendy Brown at wendywhylovesucceeds@gmail.com.

ISBN 978-0-9918414-2-4 (print)
ISBN 978-0-9918414-3-1 (ebook)

Red-hot Lover Table of Contents

Prologue to the Red-hot Lover 6

Red-hot Lover Fast Facts 10

Introduction to the Red-hot Lover 12

Section 1: Interview with Ron, a Red-hot Lover, on Red-hot Passionate Sex and Love 17

Section 2: Interview with a Red-hot Lover on Red-hot Passionate Drama 23

Section 3: Interview with a Red-hot Lover on Red-hot Passionate Chaos 30

Section 4: Red-hot Lover Test and Script 37

Section 5: Tests on the Six Passions 40

Section 6: Scripts 53

Conclusion of the Red-hot Lover 73

Our love story's a love story for the ages.

Kanye West

Prologue to the Red-hot Lover

Do you understand yourself well enough as a lover to be able to describe what kind of lover you are?

Try answering these questions:
Could you star in a great love story? Are you capable of mind-blowing sex? Would you do wild and crazy things in the name of love?

A typical Red-hot Lover will say yes to at least one of those questions.

So, what defines Red-hot Lovers?

Well, they have the capacity for super-charged sexual energy. They honor and uphold love itself. They realize that life without love can be very empty and lonely. They get carried away and do some pretty ridiculous things in the name of love. They are often misunderstood. They are capable of love affairs that rock the world: grand love stories we endlessly admire and appreciate.

Are these lovers in a gripping drama? Yes. Are they red-hot? YES.

Allow me to explain the genesis of the concept of Red-hot Love: As an individual and couples therapist, I've seen love succeed and fail. When I realized that a lot of love-life suffering is due to misinterpreting love and lovers, I decided to find a better way to understand and explain these phenomena than we have had up until now. I think we have to admit that our time-honored clichés, folk wisdom and even our therapy-based formulations leave us wanting.

I discovered that there are four different ways to think, feel and behave when you're in love. You can feel like you're in:

- A Gripping Drama

- A Passionate Adventure

- A Sensible Compromise

- A Joyful Diversion

I was inspired to write a book, Why Love Succeeds or Fails, including a test to tell you which of these types of love works for you. I proceeded to describe each of the four types and each of the ten love-matches for those types. I gave advice for how to handle your attitude to love and your love-match. I noted the red flags of each. It was my contention, and remains my contention, that love succeeds when you have enough love between you and you manage it well.

In 2014, *Why Love Succeeds or Fails* won the *National Indie Excellence Award*, for a relationship book. That made me think: Maybe I'm onto something with my taxonomy of love. After all, knowing your attitude to love tells you more about yourself than you consciously realize to be true. That gives you an edge on those who go about their love-lives in something of a semi-conscious fog. Instead, you have actual, reliable knowledge about yourself; including what is good, bad and indifferent about you. You understand that the characteristics you have that you like are probably what others find lovable about you. And the features you have that you dislike are often the same ones others find less than lovable about you.

I decided to look at each type of love again and see what more I could learn about it, starting with the first type I discovered: The Gripping Dramatist. This time, I focused on the individual lover; not the love-matches.

The Red-hot Lover is the new name I have given to the Gripping Dramatist. I previously picked up on this type's uneasiness, suspense and turmoil. I saw its primary features as sensitivity and intensity that produce a volatile love life filled with gripping drama. It is true that these lovers have gripping drama in spades. But when they're in love, they also think, feel and behave like they're red-hot.

Plus, I now realize that there are six passions of Red-hot Lovers and each of them produces a love-life script:

- Lovesick Lover

- Prince/Princess

- Lover's Fool

- White Knight

- Black Knight

The Six Passions of the Red-hot Lover

- Drama King/Queen

In case you're not Red-hot, don't despair: I will be writing books on the other three attitudes to love as well. I may even rename them as I go along.

Red-hot Lover Fast Facts

Sex: I tend to have really hot sexual energy, especially at the beginning of a relationship, in make-up sex, or after being apart. I am capable of ratcheting up my sexual tension to the point of having mind blowing sex.

Love: I can have a sensitive, heartfelt and intense emotional closeness. I have even told a select few of my lovers 'This is bigger than both of us.'

Drama: I thrive on feeling all that's sensitive, deep and intense in love relationships. The last thing I want is the emptiness and meaninglessness of a life without passion.

Chaos: My passion can be so overwhelming that I am totally blinded by it and I can't get a perspective on the situation for the life of me. I have to admit that I do have an appetite for this level of being wild and crazy at times.

Red Flags: Sex might simmer down significantly for me or even shut down for a time. I am hypersensitive to losing love. I have to be careful to avoid the drama that signals relationship trouble as opposed to the drama I thrive on. In extreme circumstances, I can have too much chaos in my life.

Passions: Typically, I have one of six passions. I may be a:

- Lovesick Lover. My passion is Heartbreak.

- Prince/Princess. My passion is Challenge.

- Lover's Fool. My passion is Pursuit.

- White Knight. My passion is Gallantry.

- Black Knight. My passion is Vindication.

- Drama King/Queen. My passion is Attention.

Our passion is our strength.

Billie Joe Armstrong

Introduction to the Red-hot Lover

Being a Red-hot Lover is quite a distinction. It means you could be one of the greatest lovers the world has ever known.

Elizabeth Taylor and Richard Burton were true Red-hot Lovers. They had the virility, the obsession, the jealousy and the pain. Liz and Dick were both married to other people when their scandalous love affair started. They received criticism from the Vatican, the US Senate and Ed Sullivan. Sixteen months after their divorce, Dick was quoted to say 'You can't keep clapping a couple of sticks [of dynamite] together without expecting them to blow up.' Whatever you think of the wild rollercoaster ride they took together, they had Red-hot Love in spades.

Of course, there are happy endings with Red-hot Love. Vivian Ward (Julia Roberts) and Edward Lewis (Richard Gere) were Red-hot Lovers in the movie *Pretty Woman*. As the picture proceeds, it becomes less and less relevant that Vivian is a prostitute. She and Edward develop a passion for each other. He ends up having his chauffeur drive him to her place in a business suit and shining car so he can climb up the fire escape (even though he's afraid of heights) with a rose in his teeth. She wanted a fairytale courtship with a knight in shining armor.

Red-hot Love has complexity to it. The Princess of Wales, Diana Spencer had the sensitivity, the anguish, the lovesickness and the drama of Red-hot Love. She lived in the realm of hope and despair; a candle in the wind.

A lot of our high maintenance drama kings and queens are Red-hot Lovers. Just think of Jackie Kennedy Onassis, who went through money and lovers like water, played a very tough game and captivated the whole world while she did it.

We need to thank lovers from the beginning of time for Red-hot Love. But, we can specifically credit the medieval courtly lovers for defining romance that's full of passion, drama, intensity and lovesickness:

- Without them we might not have drama kings and queens, princes and princesses and a lot of the high maintenance lovers of the world.

- We may have missed out entirely on the knight in shining armor rescuing the poor fellow or the damsel in distress with his/her love.

- We could be lacking the exquisitely sensitive, heartbreakingly appealing gentle lover who stumbles and falls in matters of love.

- It's possible that we wouldn't have developed the ever popular game of playing hard to get.

- And where would we be if they hadn't developed lovesickness into a prescribed ritual?

It's remarkable to see the similarities between today's Red-hot Lovers and the medieval courtly lovers. For example, Red-hot Lovers often feel like they could be members of royalty; the courtly lovers believed only the aristocracy was capable of true love. Red-hot Lovers generally have a strong sense of what's right and wrong in love; the courtly lovers had a high court of love, complete with female judges who made proclamations.

There are those who have researched the medieval period and have concluded that not only did courtly love never exist but also it was a joke. However, for the purposes of understanding Red-hot Love, it doesn't matter how much reality there was in the occurrence of courtly love. It could have been one big lie. The important fact is that we bought into it. And some of the stories from that time have a striking ring of truth to them. Whether they are a product of someone's imagination or a historical account, they are influential and powerful. For the purposes of this book, they are taken as true.

Arguably, we may not even have *Ashley Madison* if it wasn't for the courtly lovers. For all of their Courts of Love, Laws of Love, Code of Chivalry and high culture of love, they specialized in adultery. They openly promoted and condoned emotional affairs and turned a blind eye to sexual ones. They developed a system, complete with rules, for affairs. The typical love relationship was between a single gentleman and a married lady; he was probably a knight in service to her husband. When you think about the complications in that situation, it makes the drama, intrigue and betrayal in *Ashley Madison* look like a walk in the park.

And we might not even have *Tinder*.

Tinder is conceived to be exactly the opposite of what the courtly lovers were all about. They promoted one love and no sex as a means of keeping their emotions at a high pitch. But today we recognize that love is a lot of trouble: It's complicated, time-consuming and it can go wrong. Sex or a date via *Tinder* is meant to be easy: Selection is a straightforward swipe left or right, *Tinder* is instantly available on your phone and it usually produces some type of sex or date. On the surface of it, *Tinder* thumbs its nose at courtly love and Red-hot Love.

Imagine that you have the opportunity to speak with a Red-hot Lover and ask this question: So, what makes you Red-hot?

Red-hot Lover:

Passion is the key ingredient. By the way, I would define passion as either a powerful, barely controllable feeling that can overtake me at times, or a delicate, intuitive sense much like an artisan has for his/her craft. Passion is what makes me capable of mind blowing sex, sensitive close emotional attunement and anything from despair to rapture in living my life. I typically focus my passion on sex, love and drama. If I go too far with any of that, I can end up withsome measure of chaos as well.

Red-hot Love has evolved into a remarkable force of nature. It may not be the definition of chemistry between lovers, but it's certainly a contender for that role. We value it like one of the greatest natural treasures known to man. People live and die for Red-hot Love. It is a type of love unlike any other; it has a strong presence and a huge following. Arguably, it's a cultural phenomenon that we have assimilated so well that we simply take it for granted.

You might be a Red-hot Lover yourself. You can find out by:

- Reading the book, which describes this attitude to love; you'll see what features resonate with you and feel oh-so familiar, or not.

- Taking the test for the Red-hot Lover.

- Taking the tests for the six love-life scripts, which are:

    1. Lovesick Lover

    2. Prince/Princess

    3. Lover's Fool

    4. White Knight

    5. Black Knight

    6. Drama King/Queen

- Checking-out the scripts to see if you're living one or more of them.

If you're not a Red-hot Lover, you could be intrigued by someone who is one. You might just want to learn about this type of love. In any case, brace yourself:

We have a Red-hot Lover who is willing to be interviewed about what it's like to be him. The interviewer is Wendy Brown and the interviewee is Ron, a 36 year old single male and self-declared Red-hot Lover. He is a high school teacher of English Literature, with a special interest in medieval writing.

And, by the way, Red-hot Love is something to behold.

Unless it's mad, passionate or extraordinary love, it's a waste of your time. There are too many mediocre things in life; love shouldn't be one of them.

Anonymous

Section 1: Interview with Ron, a Red-hot Lover, on Red-hot Passionate Sex and Love

- **Mind-blowing Sex**
- **Falling in Love**
- **Choosing a Lover**
- **Downside to Passionate Sex and Love**

Mind-blowing Sex

Wendy: Is sex the best part of being a Red-hot Lover?

Ron: It's one of the best parts.

    The sexual passion we Red-hot Lovers experience can run the gamut from an electrifying romantic and sexual energy to a slow smoldering sensual passion. When I'm turned on by something about a person or by the feelings between us, my sexual tension can build rapidly. If the conditions are right, I can easily just let it keep heightening until everything just melds together into one hot encounter. It's like being carried on a wave that hurls me forward.

I'm honestly very pleased and proud about the fact that I'm capable of mind blowing sex. It's happened that I've just met someone and been caught off-guard by a sort of magnetic pull. Seriously, it's enough to drag a planet out of its orbit. I can also have this kind of attraction on an ongoing basis with a lover. Granted, it's usually the strongest at the beginning of our relationship, if we've been apart for a while or in make-up sex.

Falling in Love

Wendy: Do you have the same sort of powerful chemistry when you fall in love?

Ron: I have a very keen intuition and a natural affinity for sensitive, close relationships that can put my lover and me in synch. When we're on, we have a delightful connection that's deep and heartfelt.

Love empowers and emboldens me; it can be so strong that it drives me. Of course, I have daily obligations and reasons to be on my own. But I must admit that often enough I get through all of that as quickly as possible and rush over to be with my lover. I feel like she is my singular focus. We might make love, do the laundry or go for a walk. It doesn't really matter because no matter what we do, my feelings are really strong for her. I'm convinced that we're in something that's bigger than both of us.

You know, we have to thank the courtly lovers for our perspective on love. It was the troubadours who started looking at romantic and passionate love as a story that we can narrate to ourselves and others. The impact of that on us is remarkable: We're in a constant process of trying to find fulfilment by looking into ourselves and understanding our passions. We look at our lives as stories we are telling ourselves and others.

Choosing a Lover

Wendy: With love, how do you know you're on the right track with the right person?

Ron: True love gives me a feeling of dignity, respect, honor and privilege. This combination of characteristics makes me feel strong, calm and correct. I feel like this wealth of lofty emotion just keeps taking me higher and higher. It feels forever in the world like I have been elevated from having an ordinary life to one that's very extraordinary. So, when I love, I have confidence that it's the right thing to do.

I feel like this is my song when I'm in love:

Step in these arms, where you belong
It feels so right, so right
How can it be wrong?

There's something in the way you kiss
That makes me want to hold you tight
I know that nothing can't be wrong
That feels so right.

Elvis Presley song It feels so Right

This is how the medieval courtly lovers felt. They believed the passion of love was more important than life. It took their lives from black and white into color. As they developed their thoughts and feelings about love, they built in the need for great sensitivity by the gentlemen about the acceptance or rejection of the ladies. The path to success was to be immaculate about love, which made them worthy and honorable. If all proceeded as planned, eventually the lady-loves would accept the gentlemen troubadours into love service. As they tapped into the incredible force that is passionate love, they felt as though it had a real purity, more than religion. For all of that though they were still cheating. You see typically, a single gentleman or knight would choose the wife of a baron or lord as his lady-love. She would be an older woman and she could be married to his boss. They didn't marry for love; they married for property rights. Although some husbands were flattered that other gentlemen fancied their wives and others just ignored it, not everyone was OK with cheating.

Wendy: Elizabeth Taylor and Richard Burton had a recent history courtly love relationship: During the filming of Cleopatra in the early 1960's they were both married to other people and had an outrageous love affair. For the time, it was totally shocking. It included massive amounts of alcohol, fighting and lovemaking. To avoid noise complaints by hotel guests in rooms near them, they would rent the suites beside, above and below them so they could leave them empty.

Liz nearly died more than once due to illness and intentional pill overdose. Dick drank so much that his hands shook. At the end of filming, when his wife was due to collect him, the film crew ordered an ambulance to stand by in case Liz needed it.

Once the filming of *Cleopatra* was over, Liz and Dick tried to chill everything out. She said:

For four months we tried to stay away from each other. We were too aware of the pain we were causing others to stay together. But it's a hard thing to do, to run away from your fate. When you are in love and lust like that, you just grab it with both hands and ride out the storm.

The Downside to Passionate Sex and Love

Wendy: We all know that Liz and Dick didn't end up staying together. But it's hard to imagine such great passion going wrong. How could it happen?

Ron: I'm going to guess that their love finally just burnt out. I have had that happen to me. I can be totally turned on by a person or a feeling, but I can just as easily be turned right off. I don't do well if I've felt like I'm misunderstood, embarrassed or sidelined; it can give me pause.

But, even when I do love the person, it's not unusual at all for me to go from having months or years of the kind of sex most people only dream about, to none. I don't necessarily mean that there will be none ever again with my lover, but I do mean that I might bring it to a halt for a time. I don't know quite how it happens; whether my lover and I burn out all the fire or I just feel like the urgency of it has evaporated.

Managing this involves some sustained maturity on my

part. Rather than just going with the purely sexual feelings that hit me, I need to consciously use my loving feelings to produce sexual interest and momentum from the beginning of my love relationship. That may be a little lower octane than the mind-blowing kind that blind sides you, but it's really quite lovely. Then I have that process to fall back on if I fade out of the fire and urgency of it all.

Summary

Wendy: Some of the greatest love stories of all time involve Red-hot Lovers, who revel in mind-blowing sex, sensitive and close love affairs, and generally the feeling that you're in something that's bigger than both of you. They are primed to take a deep dive into being truly, deeply, madly in love. It's not just the magical, chemical combination between two people that creates this phenomenon. The individuals must have the emotional set-up in the first place that leaves them open to it: they allow themselves to be driven by passion. And although passion can be amazing, it can also be finicky and difficult at times; it can even burn out.

Imperfection is beauty, madness is genius and it's better to be absolutely ridiculous than absolutely boring.

Marilyn Munroe

Section 2: Interview with a Red-hot Lover on Red-hot Passionate Drama

- **Red-hot Passionate Drama**
- **Lovesick Lovers**
- **Princes/Princesses and White Knights**
- **Downside to Red-hot Passionate Drama**

Red-hot Passionate Drama

Wendy: You folks certainly do not avoid drama in sex, love or life. As a matter of fact, at times, you seem to be a magnet for it. What is that about?

Ron: In my mind, any great love story is loaded with drama. If my initial feelings of attraction and love are going to progress, it's because we're dealing with the drama somehow. We could live a soap opera or I alone could go from the depths of despair to the heights of rapture on a regular basis. My lover needs to jump in to the drama or help me deal with mine. You see, drama gives us the chance to explore our emotions, personalities and limits. We can experience and identify the nuances and themes of love. They fill up our emotional lives. This gives us endless opportunities to grow and change. Drama provides a lot of dynamism; it can supercharge even the most common, everyday experiences.

Even if I'm not in a relationship with a lover, I go through phases when I'm inclined towards having as much drama in my life as I can build up. Of course, I can get tired of it and chill out for a while. But, the sheer boredom of life without passion of any type will get to me.

I view drama as grist for the mill. I usually consider sensitivity, vulnerability, intensity and volatility as the drama of Red-hot Love.

Lovesick Lovers

Wendy: Why are Red-hot Lovers so in tune with lovesickness?

Ron: Lovesickness is evidence of love; it confirms that I can love, I do love and I can grieve. That's reassuring to both Red-hot Lovers and to our lovers. It gives me hope that I can continue loving someone even when the circumstances look bad. I believe it's possible for the strength of my love to turn things around. If that proves impossible, it tells me I can love again.

The courtly lovers' Laws of Love required the gentlemen to experience lovesickness as a means of tapping into the emotions of love and convincing their lady-loves of their sincerity. They believed only the aristocracy was capable of this level of depth and complex emotion.

Here's an example of super-strong internal drama due to lovesickness:

Geoffrey Rudel, a medieval troubadour prince of Blaye, a town near Bordeaux, was a very sensitive and romantic person. Not being inspired by any of the local ladies, he took a fancy to the Countess of Tripoli in Palestine, a city which had been taken by the Christians in the first Crusade. The Countess was famous for her beauty and elegance, but Geoffrey had never actually seen her. He decided to travel to Tripoli and declare his love to her directly. Alas, he didn't fare well on the trip; it appeared as though his emotions for her were overwhelming him. By the time he disembarked at Tripoli he was so agitated and worn out that he collapsed and appeared dead. He had to be carried to a house on the shore where he remained while his companions sought the Countess. She hurried to his side, just in time. He was able to sit up and hold her hand, saying 'Most illustrious princess, I will not complain of death. I have seen you, and have thus achieved the sole object, the sole desire of my life.' As she hugged him, he died. The Countess provided a tomb of porphyry for him, engraved with Arabic verses, and she had him buried among the Knights Templar at Tripoli. She ended up in such grief over him that she retreated to a nunnery.

Now I'm not about to drop dead over someone I haven't even met, but I get how the internal drama of severe lovesickness can take over a person's life.

Princes/Princesses and White Knights

Wendy: Why do Red-hot Lovers gravitate towards prince or princess roles?

Ron: Personally I relate to Princess Diana. For one thing, I feel like I can understand the love-lives of royalty. As well, she had a life that was one of the most troubling and unsettling of the Red-hot Lovers. I often feel my life is like that. Look at Princess Diana: she was a bulimic kid who married a long-time bachelor with a sterile and lonely life in the weirdness of a 20th century palace. He enjoyed hunting so much that he had his vehicle outfitted so that the blood from the animals could be easily washed off. His married mistress Camilla Parker Bowles used to kick out her husband so she could see him. Nonetheless, Diana wanted Charles to love her and tried, in her own way, to get his attention. Granted, her frustration got the better of her at times. Before the honeymoon was over, she hit him over the head with the family Bible as he knelt beside the bed saying his prayers.

In my opinion, it was the Red-hot Lover part of Diana that made her want to be a princess and kept her hanging onto the hope that Charles would love her back. When it comes to her lovesickness, I totally get it. She knew full well that he loved another woman. You could feel her suffering and her loneliness; it was totally heartbreaking. She went through years quietly looking for a knight in shining armor to rescue her with his true love.

I believe that we Red-hot Lovers actually sense our roots that go back to the courtly lovers, a thousand years ago. They were almost always members of the aristocracy. Occasionally a troubadour would be born a commoner and then obtained favor to become a knight and/or a gentleman. It was widely accepted that only the nobility was capable of understanding and appreciating love. Love, as they defined it, involved the gentleman exalting their lady-loves and everyone following the laws of love that were ordained by the jurisdictional courts of love.

Most of today's Red-hot Lovers aren't born into royalty, but it never ceases to amaze me that many of us think that we should have been. Especially when we're in love, we have a lofty celebratory feeling similar to what you might have at a coronation ceremony. Along with that we have an internal rule book that tells us what's right and wrong in matters of love; like we belong in a court of love, as a rule-maker. Altogether, this gives us a regal, privileged, rightful feeling as lovers.

Wendy: Of course, the perfect complement to the prince/princess is a white knight/rescuer.

Ron: Yes, in the Middle Ages when courtly love was in its heyday, the gentleman lover was probably a troubadour, writing songs and poetry about love. If he was also a knight, he also had to be capable of jousting and probably wore something from his lady-love, like a ribbon or a sleeve. In doing that, he showed bravery in her honor and as a means of winning her love. Thus he took on the character of a rescuer, someone who swoops in and conquers all in the name of love. Again, this is the passion of the Red-hot Lover: someone equally capable of writing sensitively, eloquently and powerfully about love and fighting with skill and valor, sometimes to the death.

There's an excellent example of a white knight in our modern-day musical *Camelot:* Lancelot. He wins at battle and wins Queen Guinevere's love. When they're caught together she is condemned to death for treason, having betrayed her husband King Arthur. Lancelot saves her from being burned at the stake.

The Downside to Red-hot Passionate Drama

Ron: Drama can signal trouble if I dislike where it takes me and I become determined not to go there anymore. My lover and I need to be attuned to the type of drama that will burn me out. The feeling of being trapped in something passionless is a feature that I personally don't take well.

Wendy: Then, of course there's internal and external drama that is distressing and disturbing. Marilyn Monroe always felt alone; she always needed rescue. She had a deep fear that she was completely empty: If she was cut open, it would be found that she was filled with finely cut sawdust, just like that in a raggedy Ann doll.

Lovesickness has defied medical science to this day. When it goes too far, it can ruin the quality of a person's life; it can even mean the end of his/her life.

Ron: I have no way of knowing if Red-hot Lovers gravitate to love-triangles any more than other lovers. But in a love-triangle, you have lots of opportunity to go through inner tumults of emotion. Your unrequited love or unsatisfied passion can build. You might live for stolen moments. You can justifiably fear that your love and your connection with your lover might be forced to end. There's the risk of being found out, which can be terrifying, upsetting and preoccupying.

This also hearkens back to the courtly lovers. They looked at it this way: You were expected to have some sort of love for your husband or wife, so that didn't count. It was only when you freely chose to love and the relationship was difficult enough to make you lovesick that you qualified as truly being in love. The Countess of Champagne actually made that ruling in her official capacity in the court of love.

Summary

Wendy: If you view sex and love as the only passions of a Red-hot Lover, you will miss out on completely understanding what makes their inner emotional lives tick. You need to see the true function and purpose of drama in their internal struggles and in their love-lives. Red-hot Lovers find fulfilment through lovesickness, prince/princess and white knight roles.

There is a caveat: Every individual and couple has a place they can go that will burn out their love. Red-hot Lovers are no different.

> *Real love is always chaotic. You lose control; you lose perspective. You lose the ability to protect yourself. The greater the love, the greater the chaos. It's a given and that's the secret.*
>
> Anonymous

Section 3: Interview with a Red-hot Lover on Red-hot Passionate Chaos

- **Red-hot Passionate Chaos**
- **The Lover's Fool**
- **Black Knights and Drama Kings/Queens**
- **Downside to Red-hot Passionate Chaos**

Red-hot Passionate Chaos

Wendy: Of all the people in the world, Red-hot Lovers are probably the most likely to experience mad, wild, crazy passions. Why are you open to that sort of chaos?

Ron: I generally trust my passions so much that I don't have mechanisms in place to correct for errors in judgment when they occur. Thus I end up driving forward, based on the feeling, with blinders on and a total inability to get a balanced perspective.

Part of the problem is I love the fact that I'm capable of letting myself go into a state of chaos over sex, love or drama. It makes me feel like I've tapped into a power source that keeps me alive and thriving. I have fond memories of saying to my lover that I'd do anything for her. I remember getting up at 5:00 am to drive for three hours so I could kiss my girlfriend before she started work. And I was on top of the world the whole time. If anybody had asked me to see her clearly, to get a balanced perspective on the situation or any other such nonsense, I wouldn't have even considered it. The feeling I had was priceless.

The Lover's Fool

Wendy: When you've been in a state of excitement and rapture, has it ever occurred to you that you could be making a fool of yourself?

Ron: No, if my lover had rejected me, I would have just kept trying. You see, in the moment I'm absolutely convinced that my passion is my guide and I can completely trust it. As a matter of fact, the stronger my passion, the bigger my blind spots and the harder it is for me to be sensible. This feeling is often quite contagious, so my lovers would frequently go from humoring me to totally buying in to the inspiration of it all.

Of all the court poets in the Middle Ages, probably the one most likely to be also named court fool was Pierre Vidal, the son of a tanner who rose to be a troubadour. He was usually very well-liked by the husbands of his lady-loves because he was no threat to them and he was enormously entertaining. At one point, he chose a lady-love by the name of Louve de Penautier; Louve means she-wolf. In his attempts to be linked with her, he asked to be called Loup, or he-wolf. One fine day he dressed himself up in wolf skins and asked the local gentlemen to hunt him on horseback with their dogs. Well, eventually the dogs caught up with him, biting him and tossing him around. When the huntsmen offered to save him, he said 'I will not allow the dogs to be driven off. I am submitting to their mangling teeth for the best of purposes.' He waited until he was half-dead so that he could show his lady-love and the world at large what he was prepared to do for love. Then he demanded to be carried to the castle of his lady-love, who couldn't help but find this more than a little amusing, as did most who heard about it. It was Louve's husband who obtained medical care for him and saw to it that he made a full recovery.

In Pierre's own words:

I have been a poor man living in a rich man's house and I have gone to the mountains and for one woman I have worn the fur of a wolf and the shepherds' dogs have run me to earth and I have been left for dead and have come back hearing them laughing

I'm not about to volunteer to be hunted with dogs, but I get the wild and crazy drive to be noticed by your lover.

Black Knights and Drama Kings/Queens

Wendy: Then, of course there were black knights among the courtly lovers.

Ron: Mordred in the musical *Camelot* would probably fit the bill as a medieval bad boy blended with a black knight. He was King Arthur's illegitimate son who came to Camelot intending to overthrow the king and claim the throne. He ensured that Arthur stayed out hunting overnight to give the lovers Queen Guinevere and Lancelot time to get together and be caught, which amounted to them committing treason. In the musical, it's clear that he feels high levels of injustice, envy and revenge.

I don't know what it feels like to want to harm others for my own gain. For me, being a black knight is more about hyper-focusing on being treated right. Imagine being lovesick on steroids that make you confrontational. I consider it to be the dark side of my passion. I could rightly or wrongly conclude that my lover is criticizing me or rejecting me in a big way and I can't take it. It might be that what's happened is just a small thing, but I panic and that puts me over the edge. I could react by calling her every minute for an hour, pacing as if I'm in a state of emergency, or convincing myself that the relationship is over and I have to move on. Of course, I want nothing more than to be totally, utterly wrong that there's a problem between us. And when we clear up whatever was causing the issue, I expect her to know I was just upset; I didn't necessarily mean what I said. That's me having a black knight experience.

Wendy: Do you understand drama kings/queens?

Ron: They're wedded to sex, love and drama but with two additional features: the gut for chaos and a liking for the focus to be squarely on them.

I've been there. Depending on my mood, I could feel like

the experience is allowing me to have a presence, to make my voice heard and possibly to be understood for this or that. I can stand on center stage and allow myself to be governed by passion.

Being a drama king or queen is something that the courtly lovers admired, fostered and enjoyed.

Wendy: There's a great illustration of a drama king and queen from the last century:

After President John F Kennedy was assassinated, the world grieved and great sympathy went out to his wife Jackie Bouvier Kennedy. When she married Aristotle Onassis, the very wealthy Greek shipping magnate, the world was shocked and horrified. As it became clearer and clearer that Jackie found Ari unattractive, hairy and uncultured, he became more and more fed up with her spending, cheating and travelling away from him. Of course, he cheated with Maria Callas and the boys he kept in different places. Jackie and Ari were relentlessly dogged by the paparazzi and Ari was forever paying them off so that they wouldn't publish embarrassing pictures of Jackie. Then, he decided to take her down a peg or two. He paid frogmen to photograph her when she was swimming nude in the waters around Skorpios, his private island, and then refused to pay to stop them. Those pictures ended up published in Hustler magazine and sold world-wide, making the magazine millions and greatly humiliating Jackie.

For all of her carrying on, which included Jackie having affairs with both of her married brothers-in law; she remains a beloved figure to many people. Like Liz Taylor, she was admired and envied for her beauty and her passions.

The Downside to Red-hot Passionate Chaos

Wendy: Do you see anything wrong with going wild and crazy with sex, love and/or drama?

Ron: Believe it or not, yes. I have had more than a few relationships fizzle out on me and I've wondered what on earth I was thinking to get so madly and passionately involved with that person in the first place. It has happened that I've been a lover's fool and lost out; then I was ridiculed for putting myself way out there on a song and a prayer.

I really seriously do not enjoy overdrive. The rest of being a black knight kind of works for me; there's an edgy side to my passion that I like to explore. I have to say I quite like most of my drama king experiences, but they can be really exhausting.

I'd say the most concerning feature of any of this for me is the blind spots, especially if they're combined with overdrive. I mean, you can get yourself into severe trouble with that. The courtly lovers thought they were developing a high class culture centered on the rapture of unrequited love. Maybe they were doing that, but they were also endorsing adultery. They had a passion-induced blind spot to the feelings of the husband of the troubadour's lady-love. Here is an example of how serious that could be:

In the 1100's, Lady Marguerita and her usher William Cabestaing were having an intensely loving affair right under the nose of her husband, Lord Raymond of Castel-Roussillon. It appeared as though Raymond loved Marguerita and was possessive over her, arranged marriage or not. Eventually, everyone in his house was talking about the affair so Raymond confronted William, who lied and got away with it. Then he made his fatal mistake: he believed he had allayed Raymond's suspicions such that they would never resurface. William then wrote a song for her, named her, and had it sung for Raymond. In all of this, William and Marguerita were behaving like true courtly lovers. But Raymond lost it and murdered them.

This is the thing about chaos; it can be high octane and high stakes.

Summary

Wendy: Chaos has great potential to be the perfect expression of passion for Red-hot Lovers. In the moment, it can provide fulfilment based on going with the feeling no matter what. It is very exhilarating, often edgy and quite distinctive. You can really say you did it your way.

But, Red-hot Lovers may or may not want to reckon with all the risks that go along with having chaos in their lives. The blind spots, errors in judgment and exposures to criticism can be hard to take.

Section 4: Red-hot Lover Test and Script

Red-hot Lover Test

Circle yes or no to the following questions:

Yes   No
Do you feel as though you can tap into the life-force that is passion?

Yes   No
Are your love relationships typically sensitive, deep, tumultuous and rapturous?

Yes   No
Is it difficult, if not impossible for you to think clearly and get a balanced perspective once your passion has been triggered?

Yes   No
Do you have a regal or majestic feeling of correctness and purpose when you fall in love?

Scoring this test:

Count your Yes answers.

Write that number here _____.

Understand your scoring:

2-4 Yes answers means you have enough characteristics for Red-hot Love that it could be a defining feature of your love-life.

0-1 Yes answers suggest that Red-hot Love is not representative of you.

It is possible, even likely, to test positive for one or more of the Six Passions if you're a Red-hot Lover.

But it is also possible to be a Red-hot Lover and not have one or more of the Six Passions.

Red-hot Lover Script

When I fall in love, I have the lofty, regal feeling of being in the right. I have to admit that I spend a lot of time in my life doing what feels right and true to me. I tap into my inner sense of what is and isn't warranted by the love I feel. When it comes to love, I have the passion of a craftsman/woman and a gifted lover. My beloved generally feels very connected to me as I thoroughly revel in the angst, drama and chaos that fill my life and make me feel fully alive and thriving. I need my lover on board, ready to explore all of that with me, at the edge of his/her seat in the excitement of it all.

I have to say, to a great extent, passion is my guide and my governor. It allows me to run the full gamut from being a vulnerable candle in the wind to a super-charged rapturous lover.

My passion does make it difficult for me to get and maintain a perspective on a given situation. Typically, I'm too busy attending to my emotions which constitute my driving force. I do realize that this means I can't see clearly or fully; I miss a lot because of that. But I love being guided by my passion so much that I really can't see myself changing.

My perfect state is being passionately in love. It makes me feel like royalty that has arrived. I am so pleased and proud that I feel like I could burst into a million glorious pieces.

Section 5: Tests on the Six Passions

- Lovesick Lover. The passion of heartbreak.
- Prince/Princess. The passion of challenge.
- Lover's Fool. The passion of pursuit.
- White Knight. The passion of gallantry.
- Black Knight. The passion of vindication.
- Drama King/Queen. The passion of attention.

Lovesick Lover Test. The passion of heartbreak.

Circle yes or no to the following questions:

Yes   No
Are you typically very sensitive, nervous and worried about your love relationships, fearing that your heart could be broken at any time?

Yes   No
Do you think that when something goes wrong between you and your lover that your lack of lovability is probably responsible for it?

Yes   No
Are you inclined to be very self-critical over your wrongdoing if you somehow upset or offend your lover?

Yes   No
Do you tend to jump from feeling disappointed or hurt to concluding that your relationship is over?

Scoring this test:

Count your Yes answers.

Write that number here _____.

Understand your scoring:

2-4 Yes answers means you have enough characteristics for this passion that it could be a defining feature of your love-life.

0-1 Yes answers suggest that this passion is not representative of you.

It is possible to test positive for more than one passion.

Prince/Princess Test. The passion of challenge.

Circle yes or no to the following questions:

Yes   No
Deep down do you feel as though you were always meant to be royalty, or at least treated like royalty in your love-life?

Yes   No
If something goes wrong between you and your lover, do you need considerable support, gentleness and even pampering to prevent you from being heartbroken?

Yes   No
Do you feel as though you have every right in the world to be treated like you are the centre of your lover's universe?

Yes   No
Are you likely to be hotly offended and justifiably outraged if your lover does something inconsiderate or self-centered?

Scoring this test:

Count your Yes answers.

Write that number here _____.

Understand your scoring:

2-4 Yes answers means you have enough characteristics for this passion that it could be a defining feature of your love-life.

0-1 Yes answers suggest that this passion is not representative of you.

It is possible to test positive for more than one passion.

Lover's Fool Test. The passion of pursuit.

Circle yes or no to the following questions:

Yes   No
Do you tend to fall head over heels in love and get completely carried away by your feelings of love?

Yes   No
Are you inclined to gloss over details like how your lover is responding to your advances?

Yes   No
Do you think you need to make grand gestures and really go to town in demonstrating how you feel when you're in love?

Yes   No
Are you convinced that you will somehow win over your lover if you fervently believe in the strength of your feelings and proudly make your case to the world?

Scoring this test:

Count your Yes answers.

Write that number here _____.

Understand your scoring:

2-4 Yes answers means you have enough characteristics for this passion that it could be a defining feature of your love-life.

0-1 Yes answers suggest that this passion is not representative of you.

It is possible to test positive for more than one passion.

White Knight Test. The passion of gallantry.

Circle yes or no to the following questions:

Yes   No
Have you always felt like you could be a hero?

Yes   No
If you feel like your lover is in distress, does it feel like your heart will burst if you can't help him/her?

Yes   No
Do you think that, to an extent, you prove yourself worthy to your lover when you do something courageous or loving?

Yes   No
When you have a lover, do you feel as though you have purpose and meaning in your life?

Scoring this test:

Count your Yes answers.

Write that number here _____.

Understand your scoring:

2-4 Yes answers means you have enough characteristics for this passion that it could be a defining feature of your love-life.

0-1 Yes answers suggest that this passion is not representative of you.

It is possible to test positive for more than one passion.

Black Knight Test. The passion of vindication.

Circle yes or no to the following questions:

Yes   No
Do you tend to go into an all-out panic if you rightly or wrongly conclude your lover is too busy for you, may be thinking about somebody else or simply stopped loving you?

Yes   No
If you're feeling at risk of losing love, do you become hyper focused on it; so much so that you can't think of anything else and you feel enormous dread?

Yes   No
Do you become obsessed with needing to contact your lover for reassurance?

Yes   No
Are you inclined to say things to your lover that you may seriously regret later; that-is be very critical or even threatening of him/her or yourself?

Scoring this test:

Count your Yes answers.

Write that number here _____.

Understand your scoring:

2-4 Yes answers means you have enough characteristics for this passion that it could be a defining feature of your love-life.

0-1 Yes answers suggest that this passion is not representative of you.

It is possible to test positive for more than one passion.

Drama King/Queen Test. The passion of attention.

Circle yes or no to the following questions:

Yes   No
Do you realize that you actually have quite a liking for being on center stage?

Yes   No
When all eyes are on you, does it give you a feeling of inner calm because that's how it should be, along with a feeling of inner tension because you want to look good?

Yes   No
Do you have a strong sense that you need to prove yourself through pushing for what you want and demanding recognition as an important person who should get it?

Yes   No
When you are trying to make your point about the importance of this or that in your life, do you develop and express some pretty over the top thoughts and feelings?

Scoring this test:

Count your Yes answers.

Write that number here _____.

Understand your scoring:

2-4 Yes answers means you have enough characteristics for this passion that it could be a defining feature of your love-life.

0-1 Yes answers suggest that this passion is not representative of you.

It is possible to test positive for more than one passion.

If the script is good, everything you need is there. I just try and feel it and do it honestly.

Olivia Coleman

Section 6: Scripts

- **Lovesick Lover**
- **Prince/Princess**
- **Lover's Fool**
- **White Knight**
- **Black Knight**
- **Drama King/Queen**
- **Generic Red-hot Lover**

You basically fall into thinking, feeling and behaving in a particular way when you're in love. You don't realize it but along the way you make decisions about yourself and your life as a lover. When you do this, you basically set yourself up with a script to follow in your love-life. It's like having a script in a movie; it tells you the actions to take and the path to follow.

If you have a script, you may not be able to identify it on your own. It's very difficult to be able to get a perspective on your inner thoughts and feelings, plus your actions over the long term. But, once it's pointed out to you, you'll probably be able to see that the beginning, middle and end of some of your love relationships are remarkably similar. Your preoccupations and conclusions about love will also tend to focus on certain elements. Even if you have a script, it won't necessarily govern you in all your love relationships. It's entirely possible that you have more than one, or one primary and one secondary. One may be in the Red-hot Lover group and one may be in another group. There are four types of love:

- Red-hot Love (originally called Gripping Drama)
- Passionate Adventure
- Sensible Compromise
- Joyful Diversion

Lovesick Lover Script

The Lovesick Lover

I'm all about making the grade as a valued lover. Picture me holding a daisy, pulling out a petal and saying 'He/she loves me'. Then with another petal I say 'He/she loves me not.' I'm keenly aware that my lover could love me and leave me, or be proven to have never loved me at all. I feel very vulnerable as I wait for both my lover's vote of approval and my feeling of confidence to go along with it.

Toward that end, I evaluate myself and my interactions with my lover to see if we have enough love, the right type of love and whether or not it's the kind of love each of us needs. It's exhausting, but the alternative is worse: Me feeling like I have little ability to understand or predict my love relationship; me running the risk of developing a false sense of happiness and security; and me fearing a big thud down the road.

To be one step ahead of the game, I keep a secret storehouse of worries, fears and dreads about my lover and my love life. So, when my lover and I have a difference of some sort, I refer back to my top concerns for a possible explanation.

Being preoccupied like this means I'm forever teetering on the edge of lovesickness. If I find an actual problem, I'm poised to go full tilt into heartbreak.

The downside and upside of being a Lovesick Lover

Unfortunately, I feel that I have to focus on all the flaws and problems with my lover and our love relationship. I might even unintentionally exaggerate some and dream up a few that might be on their way into our lives. So, I can become terribly upset for no good reason. And I'm blinded to a lot of the redeeming features we have.

If I engage my lover in any of this lovesick thinking and feeling, he/she might try to be understanding and supportive, at least for a while. But, generally that doesn't last; he/she expects me to rally and drop the concerns. When I can't, he/she might tell me I'm a wet blanket and I need to develop some joie de vivre.

This may sound odd, but it gives me a feeling of being in control to be a Lovesick Lover. I feel so terrible when I'm fretting, worrying and panicking that I don't think I could feel any worse no matter what happened. Going through this also keeps me humble and grounded.

Let's suppose I experience terrible feelings of grief and loss and I feel totally sick at heart. Then my love relationship survives: I have a wonderful, exhilarating feeling of relief and gratitude. I feel like

I've confirmed my worth, my lover's worth and the worth of our love relationship.

My historical roots

Lovesickness has been around as long as romantic and passionate love has existed in this world. For the medieval courtly lovers, it became an essential part of courtship.

The unmarried knight would admire the wife of his liege lord from afar. Typically, he would see her as beautiful, graceful and superior. He would be filled with the hopes, dreams and wishes that one day she would return his love. However, as a married woman, she could not be too open or easily won over. The gentleman lover would experience lovesickness: feeling faint, having heart palpitations, changes of color, chills, fevers, aches and insomnia. Jealousy was considered to be essential. All of this misery was evidence of love. So, there was no pleasure without pain. But the knight was not to suffer in vain. By his suffering through lovesickness, bravery in battle and honor in following the Laws of Love, he would purify himself and his status would increase to her level. In other words, he would progress from being an unworthy lover to a worthy one. Then his lady love was obliged to eventually take him into love service. But even then, their relationship wasn't meant to be public knowledge; nor was it to be consummated. Of course, in practice, there were exceptions. Sometimes a husband was flattered that a troubadour wrote about adoring his wife. And there were lovers who were physically intimate. But the lovers were supposed to maintain a sort of secret frustrated longing for each other; that was set up primarily to keep their love alive and thriving.

The passion of heartbreak

I realize that it sounds strange to be passionate about lovesickness and having your heart broken. But I have a serious problem with the feelings I have when someone loses love for me. It messes with my ability to trust and feel secure. I ask myself what I've done wrong, what he/she has done wrong and how our errors and omissions could become so serious and so final that they could end our love. Then, I need to know if it's really over, or if our love can be resumed. I find myself deeply involved in trying to get a handle on this from the beginning. At best it gives me strength; at worst it provides some solace.

Prince/Princess Script

I'm relieved and enthralled when my lover takes up the challenges I put out there. Think of me as Bambi standing on unsteady legs on the ice. I have big-eyed wonder and an impressionable heart. My lover needs to make sure I don't end up disappointed and hurt.

First and foremost, I need to be able to trust my lover enough that I'm OK letting him/her in on my secret fears and worries. Often they center on the fact that I can't get what I want and need on my own. It might be a material advantage, a preferred position in society or confirmation that I'm lovable and desirable. I also tend to be concerned about the risk of being taken for granted, viewed as commonplace, or expected to compromise my standards. When my lover is generous and/or rescues me from whatever is frightening me, I see him/her as understanding, kind and supportive. That means lovable.

But, it's still difficult for me to drop my guard and open up my heart. To do that, I have to give up the regal sort of distance and superiority I maintain. I feel like I have to give in to love. My lover needs to impress me with his/her love, plus help me have confidence that he/she can see me clearly, challenge my emotional reclusiveness and still enchant me. That's a pretty tall order and it's not surprising that few lovers accomplish all of it.

The downside and upside of being a Prince/Princess

I don't take competition very well. Generally other Princes/Princesses understand me, as do those who feel indulgent towards me. But most people who use other methods than mine to seek and obtain lovers often have a hard time with me. They've accused me of trying to be superior and playing hard to get. The truth is that I actually feel very vulnerable and I'm not really playing hard to get. I am hard to get because I'm complex and guarded.

Probably the worst experience for me comes from the lover who is intrigued and inspired by me, but primarily sees me as a conquest. He/she just wants to win my heart and walk away with that victory in hand. In my mind, he/she misses the point: This isn't all about power. Plus, he/she takes advantage of the fact that I can be hurt.

Most of the time I love being a Prince/Princess because there's so much in the role that reminds me love is grand. Imagine being at the center of your lover's world; he/she is ready to climb the tallest mountain or swim the deepest sea for you. It is life and love affirming to have someone proving his/her love; it makes you feel totally safe and utterly exhilarated opening up to it.

My historical roots

Our concept of princes/princesses comes from the history books and the imaginations of authors who have written fictional accounts of them and fairy tales about them. Significant for this script are the medieval aristocratic women who had courtly lovers. Their culture taught them to behave in a haughty and difficult fashion with their prospective lovers; they needed to come across as unattainable, arrogant and elite. After all, they were married and their propriety could be questioned if they were easily engaged by their gentlemen lovers.

Bear in mind that medieval antifeminism was the norm for most people, but not for the courtly lovers: the majority of the aristocrats in parts of what are now France and England. Women outside this group were often treated poorly, disrespectfully and even violently. For example, they had no importance in the Church. The focus was on men to be devout, to sacrifice and to submit to religion and to God. It was hoped that they would abstain from sex as much as possible. Even the development of Mariolatry, worship of the Virgin Mary, was not to the liking of many Churchmen. And it was no better outside the Church. In the 1100's, Walter Map wrote to a friend 'The very best woman (who is rarer than the phoenix) cannot be loved without the bitterness of fear, anxiety and frequent misfortune.' As a final example: If a knight found a peasant woman beautiful, he was not expected to woo her; he was told to just force himself upon her.

Then, along came the troubadours who adored the ladies of the court; they saw them as lovely, superior, desirable and enchanting. These women lived in a bubble of social approval and liberty which allowed them to have both husbands and secret lovers. This was reinforced by the Courts of Love, which were run by women such as Queen Eleanor of Aquitaine and her daughter the Countess of Champagne. But none of that gave them a tremendously strong social or legal position should they be seriously challenged. For example, Queen Eleanor of Aquitaine found herself imprisoned in a tower by her husband.

The passion of challenge

Everything about me is a challenge: Understanding me, getting close to me, holding my interest, providing me with excitement. My passion is focused on those who take the bait. I ask myself if it's really possible that someone has all the features and nuances I need to become fully engaged with him/her. I find this process endearing, heartening and exciting. You see, deep down I wonder if I really deserve all of this. But as I see my lover ticking all the boxes and my heart softening to him/her, I realize that we deserve each other.

Lover's Fool Script

Let's suppose I'm dead wrong about my love interest's feelings about me. For argument's sake, presume he/she is not attracted to me and doesn't want to pursue a relationship with me at all. (I know that's hard to believe, but stretch your imagination.) I ignore all of that because I have the inkling from somewhere that I should just put blinders on and plow forward. There are those who see me as a fool for doing that, but I have confidence in the dynamic of pursuit. Sometimes my lover is flattered, impressed and heartened by my drive and persistence and I succeed.

My passion is about marching to my own drummer in single-mindedly pursuing my chosen lover and paying no heed to the resistance I encounter along the way. I might pick up the fact that my potential lover has insecurities about whether or not he/she is lovable. Perhaps not enough pursuers have been strong and determined in paying him/her attention. Maybe they've had too many inhibitions and haven't made their advances completely clear. It's even possible that my beloved doesn't think I'm the one for him/her. I reject that notion because for my passion to have been triggered, I must have picked up some attraction or interest from him/her.

I realize that I may sound presumptuous or overly confident, but I believe that my feelings of passion are my best guide. By the way, I often succeed with lovers who are way more attractive, accomplished and/or amazing than I am. If I was wedded to being reasonable, logical and humble, I would never think I had a chance with these people.

The downside and upside of being a Lover's Fool

Probably the worst part of my role as a Lover's Fool is that I am often misunderstood. There are people who accuse me of being tuned-out when I receive feedback or criticism that goes against my objectives. I realize that some of them laugh at me because I seem to be missing a lot of clues and hints. Here's the truth: I get it, but I let most of it bounce off of me. I'm constantly in the process of stripping down the reality in front of me to make it into something I can work with. I'm ruled by passion, not by the semi-useful thoughts and feelings from potential lovers who come my way. Some of them are random and others are off-base. I feel strongly that I need to remain tapped in to my feelings of passion in the hopes that I can inspire others to jump on the bandwagon with me.

The most amazing and wonderful feature of being a Lover's Fool is the sheer gratification I feel from being proven right. It's like I've had to lead a charge and keep everybody's momentum up for the duration. And then it turns out that I was a good leader, maybe even a great leader, using passion as my guide and single-minded persistence as my modus operandi.

My historical roots

The fool has a long history, going back to ancient times. Fools included philosophers, poets, minstrels and jesters, mostly but not exclusively men. Fools are those with the ability to see what is not obvious and put it forward to produce laughter and thought. They were often at odds with their social group, but they might reach a person here or there who would see their wit and wisdom. At best, these individuals had the freedom of speech enjoyed by our modern day press and their deaths were mourned by those they amused. At worst, they risked torture and death at the hands of an offended power mad patron.

At the time of the courtly lovers, Pierre Vidal was well known as a troubadour and a fool. He was very capable as both poet and prankster. It was said of Pierre that he was 'one of the most foolish men who ever lived, for he believed everything to be just as it pleased him and as he would have it.' He fell in love with every lady he met and believed his personal appeal was so strong that it made him totally irresistible. He said, in verse, that all husbands were afraid of him more than fire or sword. This is interesting because most of the ladies' husbands actually liked him and found him entertaining. Often, the ladies would roll their eyes at him.

Barral, the Viscount of Baux, took to Pierre to the extent that he made him a constant guest at the castle. Pierre, of course, fell in love with Barral's wife, Azalais and wrote poetry to her using the name Vierna for her. Jealousy was the farthest thing from Barral's mind; he went out of his way to demonstrate that he maintained a bond of brotherhood with Pierre. He provided him with armor and clothing so like his own that from a distance they looked like twins. They went by the same name, ate, drank and hunted together. Pierre decided to take advantage of the situation: he went to Azalais' bedchamber when she was asleep, dressed like her husband, and woke her up with a kiss. He fully expected that she would allow him to go further, misperceiving him as Barral. However, instead she screamed and carried on until he was forced to run out. Barral, ever on Pierre's side, did his best to defuse the situation and represent it as a harmless practical joke. But, the lady's indignation was too great for that; eventually Pierre was forced to leave that part of the country.

At the end of his many exploits, Pierre wrote:

I won and I won and all the women in the world
were in love with me and they wanted what I wanted
so I thought and every one of them deceived me
I was the greatest fool in the world I was the world's fool

The passion of pursuit

I liken my passion to that of a great war hero who had to make decisions under pressure with few resources and needed to largely trust his/her gut. My ultimate experience is in that moment of reckoning when I realize I have nothing but a song and a prayer and the culmination of my deepest and strongest feelings. I realize that I can win big and I can lose big. But, no matter what happens within me I know that I had what it took to give chase, to pursue like no one has pursued before.

White Knight Script

For me, the feeling of being a champion is very similar to the feeling of being in love. Think of me in full armor on a white charger, lance in hand, and ready to rescue the prince/princess from the tower. I'm literally riding high, feeling exhilarated. I see this moment as the peak of my life's work; it represents everything I stand for and all I've worked hard to achieve.

I embrace the whole concept of gallantry. Not only do I have bravery, heroism and grit, but also respect and propriety. I realize with every fiber of my being that I have to fight to uphold my ideals.

As I swoop in to save the day, I figure that I prove myself worthy of love. After all, I'm going full tilt being a hero, as one in a long line of honorable, chivalrous dragon-slayers. I do the right thing to the best of my ability, so my motives should be beyond question. I am in a strong moral position to be trusted with the responsibility of taking charge. It's usually a lot of work, requiring considerable bravery and fortitude plus great sacrifice on my part. So, although I try to be humble, I accept respect and gratitude quite well; I'm also good with love and admiration. At the end of the day, I see myself rescuing my lover from a life without my love and protection.

The downside and upside of being a White Knight

Of course, I have been accused of being on a power trip with my superior white knight attitude. I do have the belief that I'm worthy, lovable and deserving due to my commitment to all my high-minded endeavors. That goes a long way to remove any doubt or anxiety I might have about myself. It does make it difficult for me to keep a perspective on myself and my rescues. I guess there are times I can be legitimately accused of being controlling; maybe even full of myself.

Usually, my lovers at least initially appreciate and respect me, plus accord me some loyalty. I understand that it can be tiresome to have me eternally taking over and trying to affect a rescue of some sort. Most people want to have a say about the kind of heroism they receive, how much and over what issues.

My bottom line is that I'm a proud and dignified person with a strong personal code. I feel pretty good about myself when I'm in rescue mode or when I have the opportunity to be the bigger person. I find it absolutely glorious to come in for my victory lap, having saved the day and won the lover of my dreams.

My historical roots

The White Knight is the quintessentially sensitive, loving, gallant brave figure in fairy tale and legend. Traditionally, this is the prince who rescues his lady-love in the tower.

In medieval France and England, courtly love developed a foothold in the upper classes for several centuries. The troubadours could be aristocratic, wealthy men or they could be of lowly birth or means and be supported by a noble. In either case, they probably were fully accomplished knights who were compelled to follow the Code of Chivalry.

The word troubadour comes from the concepts of finding, music, love and ardor. Typically, the troubadours had high ideals and promoted a spirit of equality among people based on character and actions. They tended to play down the importance of blood and wealth. The troubadours are best known for their poetry and songs, many of which have been preserved to this day.

Following the tradition of the knights-errant, the troubadours would travel from castle to castle with their entourage of jongleurs who were singers and musicians. When a troubadour would arrive at a castle in full armor on horseback, the servants and ladies would help him undress down to a thin tunic. They would have a mantle ready for him, trimmed with fur, gold and embroidery. The troubadour would stay for days, weeks or months. He might only sing or recite poetry. But if the troubadour was a knight, the liege lord might also host a tournament, which would be held in a field near the castle. Both nobility and commoners would attend the very festive, highly decorated event which could last for days. Knights would engage in a series of combats, like jousting, wearing something from their respective lady-loves. For example, he could attach his lady's veil or ribbon to his arm or to his lance. This was a way for him to show bravery and valor to prove he was worthy to win or keep her heart.

The passion of gallantry

I am greatly inspired by capturing the moment in which I decide to be a hero, someone with a noble calling and the capacity for glory. It is my passion to find that spark within myself and go with it. I feel as though I become greater than the sum of my parts. I have something that's almost magical within my grasp and I am capable of commandeering it for the greater good.

Black Knight Script

The springboard for my passion comes from the feeling of perfect love I have at the beginning of my love relationship. That's my birthright and I'm sensitive to any interference with it. If it's somehow displaced or reduced, I develop a strong sense of disappointment and injustice. At those times, I can't help but feel some rebellion, even outrage. I find it essential to right the wrong against me, obtain vindication and restore the love I need.

Even if I say so myself: I have amazing abilities when it comes to sensitivity, openness, caring and acceptance. Mine is a delicate, intuitive sense which tends to produce a lot of intimacy. This is my passion and my pride. Picture me as the regal male peacock with my feathers on display. My lover is usually very touched and deeply moved by the exquisite quality of our connection. It goes a long way to bond us emotionally.

I know I can be faulted for having a strong reaction when something goes wrong; it feels like the spell is broken and can't be re-established. That throws me for a loop and then I rebel. I don't want to accept a lesser life or a lesser love. I need to make it absolutely clear that I deserve better than that. I'm outraged that I have to feel lovesick, which I find acutely painful, and I don't want to continue down that path. So, I go into overdrive in which I fight desperately to redeem myself, repair my relationship and eliminate the need for lovesickness. If I'm very lucky, my overdrive comes across as edgy, racy and sexy. If I'm not so lucky, I can look pretty troubled, possibly needy.

The downside and upside of being a Black Knight

Even at the height of my passion, when my relationship is wonderful, there's a small part of me that's vigilant. I'm anticipating at any time I may be misunderstood, overlooked, sidelined and ignored by my lover.

Generally speaking, I am very sensitive about anything and everything that goes awry. I quickly and easily feel out of sorts, uncomfortable and insecure. Often enough, my pride gets involved and I keep feeling as though my lover needs to give me a chance. I might work myself up enough to feel frantic, sick to my stomach and tormented by this thought or that feeling. I'm hyper-sensitive to anything and everything my lover does to confirm our relationship is flawed. I desperately want him/her to change that assessment. I don't want the spell to be broken; I can't rest until it's repaired and restored by apologies and no hard feelings.

When I've been overly critical and hard to please too many times, my lover usually becomes scared about it happening again and again. Alternatively, he she might just get very fed up.

But, allow me to say, bearing all of that in mind, I have no shortage of lovers. I find a lot of people gravitate to me instinctively; they pick up my superior abilities when it comes to emotional and physical intimacy. It produces the amazing and wonderful intermingling of love and passion that feels almost perfect.

My historical roots

Historically, the black knight is a person who is somehow disenfranchised and outraged over it. He/she is committed to right the wrong done to him/her by fair means or foul. His/her goal is obtaining or restoring the position, freedom, or power that will relieve the injustice or unfairness.

In the medieval period, it had already become apparent to Churchmen and liege lords that knights had to be corralled and controlled; otherwise they had a lot of power as fighters who could take up the cause of their self-interest. They were often feared by the peasant population because at the end of a battle, they would loot and pillage whatever they needed and rape women as they felt like it. Thus, the Code of Chivalry was developed and knights were bound by their honor to uphold it.

The life of a knight wasn't always wonderful. If he was not the first born son of his aristocratic and wealthy parents, he wouldn't inherit money and land. If he was supported by the generosity of a wealthy gentleman, he would be subject to his whims and decisions. It was entirely possible that the knight could be injured or killed when he was jousting or fighting. There are even stories of knights stealing the armor and munitions of their fellow knights when they were incapacitated.

Then, of course, life wasn't really easy with their lady-loves. The Courts of Love went to great lengths to ensure that the women treated their gentlemen lovers respectfully and fairly, but some still took advantage of the troubadours who had to prove themselves by suffering lovesickness and sometimes real hardship.

Camelot is a modern-day musical about the mythical medieval kingdom of King Arthur. When his illegitimate son Mordred arrived at Camelot Arthur invited him to be a Knight of the Round Table. But he said he hated swards, spears and horses; he didn't understand or accept virtues. Arthur wanted to work with him, his only son, so that one day he could take the throne. However in the meantime Mordred recruited banished knights to help him destroy the Round Table and take the throne. They succeeded in literally breaking the table into pieces.

Everyone knew that Arthur's favorite Knight Lancelot and his Queen Guinevere were having an affair and Mordred decided to exploit the situation. He convinced Arthur to stay out hunting in the forest overnight to give the lovers the opportunity to get together. As they walked arm in arm Mordred and other knights accused them of treason and they captured Guinevere. She was imprisoned, tried and sentenced to burn at the stake. Almost everyone including Arthur hoped that Lancelot would be able to rescue her. The one exception was Mordred who mocked Arthur by saying 'Let her die, your life is over. Let her live, your life's a fraud. Kill the Queen or kill the law.'

The passion of vindication

Imagine that you're holding a wonderful, amazing trophy that fills you with rapture and joy. Then, right before your eyes, it starts to tarnish and decay. You have the utmost feeling of horror and dismay. But, instead of just standing idly by allowing this devastating event to occur, you do everything in your power to restore the trophy. Being frantic and desperate, you don't necessarily use the best methods and you might not put yourself in the best light. However, your passion is fixed on the perfection of the trophy which represents your love; it's the deepest, best part of you. Vindication of that is your single-minded goal.

Drama King/Queen Script

I can tell you that I thrive on certain types of attention. I'm good with being treated like visiting royalty or the star of the show. I adore being the center of my lover's world. It's great if he/she can intuit my wants and needs. But I'm also fine with emphatically expressing my innermost thoughts and feelings, knowing I have someone deeply invested in keeping my sense of well-being intact. Receiving the precise type of attention I need gives me a magnificent feeling of delight; it's an indulgence but it's one I need.

Along with this, I have the indelible knowledge that I should have been born into the monarchy. You see, it's usually only royalty that receives undivided attention and the concerted effort to please him/her at any cost. It's under those conditions that I would flourish. I know lots of people who would dislike that level of individual focus and distrust the sincerity of the individuals trying to make the king/queen happy. However I feel as though I would be able to work well within that system because I would feel seen and heard. My greatest fear in life is being invisible.

So, I start to feel slightly perturbed if I conclude that I'm not being recognized and appreciated, especially by my lover. I feel as though he/she loves me and knows how important it is for me to have an acknowledged presence, visibility of my emotional needs and solid effort to provide me with nurture.

The downside and upside of being a Drama King/Queen

In all honesty, I don't understand why anyone wouldn't want to give me the opportunity to have the spotlight on me. I mean, there are lots of people who shrink away from that sort of exposure, who dislike center stage. I, on the other hand, thrive on it and I'm willing to even share it sometimes. So, for reasons I don't completely understand, I've been told to take it elsewhere, that I'm high maintenance or it's all about me.

I generally come on the scene as a person with a purpose, a destiny to fulfill and hunger to satisfy. I gravitate to the spot where I'm appreciated and understood. That usually involves me receiving a fair bit of attention from my lover and being given the license to revel in my new-found dynasty of emotional support.

As life happens and I lose my primacy in the eyes of my lover, I become notably discontented. I feel a strong lack of fit with the change and I usually seek to correct the situation. Perhaps I can't restore the wonder and bliss of new love, but I can get the focus back on me somehow. I have a lot of capability when it comes to being dramatic and expressive and I use it.

My historical roots

From the beginning of time, there have been individuals who have gravitated to roles of primary importance and high visibility. Center stage seems to feed their insatiable hunger for position and/or prominence. They have the uncompromising need for validation.

In the courtly love period, the nobility highly valued dramatic expression of love, even if it became an exaggerated affectation. This reinforced their central belief that people needed to be all in when it came to love. It also recognized the standing of the lady-loves. In general, the women could be very haughty and difficult to their gentlemen lovers in the initial stages of courtship. They were expected to look like they had no intention of having emotional affairs and dishonoring their husbands. The gentlemen suitors likewise could go to great lengths in their expressions of lovesickness to prove the case that their love was real and should be accepted. In the moment, this could represent a standoff between a drama queen and a drama king. In their culture at the time, they would not have been seen as self-serving; they were serving love.

This is a great example of a drama king and queen: When the courtly lover Richard de Barbesieu was turned away by the Countess of Touai, he moved on to another lady-love who accused him of being unfaithful to the Countess and insisted he return to her. When the Countess continued to play hard to get and rejected him again, he decided to follow the model of the monks and friars: he became a hermit in a hut in the forest. This would be considered to be an exaggerated affectation but totally in keeping with his role as a lovesick suitor. By the time he had done this for two years however, concerned friends began talking with him and the Countess, encouraging them to end this stalemate. Eventually the Countess said if one hundred ladies and one hundred gentlemen who were in love came to her holding hands and fell on their knees in front of her, she would pardon the troubadour. They complied and the issue was resolved.

The passion of attention

Just picture of me in the spotlight; all eyes are on me as I explore how I think and feel. My audience expects me to be extraordinary. I can probably even get away with being excessive and overdone. You see my admirers get caught up in my internal drama, which makes me interesting, entertaining and inspiring. Forever in the world, having that sort of riveting attention is my passion and my purpose. It gives me a feeling of primacy and majesty to hold that place on center stage.

*There is no passion to be found in playing small-in settling for
a life that is less than the one you are capable of living*

Nelson Mandela

Conclusion of the Red-hot Lover

Let me begin by commenting that there is no conclusion to the incredible phenomenon that is Red-hot Love. It is alive and well among us and will remain so.

Red-hot Lovers are passion-seekers; they are passion-lovers. Sex, love, drama and chaos are all within their repertoire of ways to experience and thrive on passion. The lovers are able to shut out the rest of the world and just focus on each other. You can feel their passion in the air, see it in them and forever in the world it feels like a force the lovers and everyone else must reckon with. You have probably heard them say 'This is bigger than both of us.' And you've seen these Red-hot Lovers justify their title as the quintessential great lovers of all time. They have the sensitivity, delicacy, meaning and purpose, plus drive and intensity. This is their passion for love and life.

For a moment, consider the depth and breadth of the cultural phenomenon that is Red-hot Love. We view our love lives in the tradition started by the troubadours. We tell the narrative about how we think, feel and behave when we're in love and how our lovers respond. The scripts of Red-hot Lovers are played out every day and everywhere you turn. And there's a never-ending stream of new recruits jumping on the bandwagon.

We are emotionally attached to our Red-hot Lovers:

Just think about lovesickness, the heartbreak and grief of lost love. It's a powerful state of mind; it has defied medical science to this day. The writers of songs, poems and books have tried to relish in it, dispel it and explain it. Friends and family do their best to understand it and help the lovelorn through the pain of it. The courtly lovers produced a prototype Lovesick Lover in the troubadour who was expected to experience the tenderness and vulnerability of heartbreak when he was rejected by his lady love. Being married, she was compelled to at least appear to be unattainable for a lengthy period of time in their courtship. In response, the troubadour would go into full scale lovesickness to prove his love and to prepare for the ultimate heartbreak that may be coming. However, he would hold out hope that the strength of his love could make her change her mind and relieve him of his lovesickness. The Red-hot Lovesick Lover is steeped in this tradition; he/she is passionately tied to how and why lovers lose love for each other and whether or not the appearance of lost love is real.

Now, the game of playing hard to get is so much a part of our culture that we don't even think twice about it. For many people, it's just what you do when you want to save face, receive an ego boost or put someone in his/her place.

But those who casually play the game may not be true dyed in the wool princes/princesses. Think of the medieval Princess; courtly love dictated that she hold back from a lover until he proved himself worthy. If she was married, she needed to at least appear to be guided by propriety and give in to love only when it was abundant and secret. A Red-hot Lover Prince/Princess really is hard to get because he/she has a list of complex needs and a real fear of being let down. His/her passion is centered on putting forward challenges to potential lovers, knowing that only those with the right mix of characteristics and a lot of love will succeed. Then and only then will the Prince/Princess give up his/her emotional reserve and open up to love.

Then, what about the person who develops a thing for you that makes no sense to anyone except him/her. And, he/she just keeps it coming. You could be flattered, annoyed or just plain incredulous. It may be that not many potential lovers have had his/her level of confidence and persistence with you. Consider the classic fool of the court who was lauded for his ability to jest and comment based on insight and perceptiveness. He needed to be able to see what others didn't and hold onto his perspective as the audience laughed at and ridiculed him. Every now and then he would be credited with seeing or feeling something the others missed. The Red-hot Lover's Fool follows this model; employing his/her passion for pursuit, sometimes against all odds, based on his/her ability to trust his/her feelings. This individual may very well suffer rejection in spades, but every now and then he/she can win out and win big.

How many of our fairy tales, movies, plays and books revolve around the knight in shining armor? This hero can be male, female, human, non-human and super-human. We love him/her for having courage, taking risks and doing what's right by love. This is a pillar of our culture: the classic rescuer. In the courtly love period, this was the troubadour, often a fully accomplished knight, who participated in tournaments, plus wrote poetry to his lady love. Lancelot in the musical Camelot was just such a romantic figure, dear and trusted friend of King Arthur. Lancelot fell in love with Arthur's wife Queen Guinevere. Like any white knight, he was wedded to the concept of gallantry. It inspired and compelled him to save Guinevere from being burned at the stake. This is the passion of the Red-hot Lover White Knight, who wants to slay the dragon, prove his/her love and save the day. He/she is deeply tied to his/her ideals of courage, dignity and correctness.

What about the bad boy/girl who has exactly the right mix of sensitivity, connectedness and edginess? This is the person who somehow ends up misunderstood, on the outs and disenfranchised. And our hearts go out to him/her in his/her anguished struggle to be restored and redeemed, even if we feel he/she goes too far. Mordred, from the musical Camelot, is hell bent on destroying his father King Arthur's Round Table and ultimately his kingship. The Red-hot Lover Black Knight has the passion of vindication, wanting to have the perfect love and the best bond with his/her lover. With every fiber of his/her being, he/she wants the bubble to never burst and the spell to never break.

Then, there are our drama kings/queens who take center stage and keep us captive by seeming larger than life. These are people who relish in sharing as they go about exploring their thoughts and feelings. Consider the monarch who has all the members of the court waiting for his/her next word, hoping that they can figure out how to best serve him/her. In the courtly love period, drama kings and queens were accepted without much ado or criticism unless they went too far. Sometimes a lovesick troubadour would show the depth and breadth of his love by wearing summer clothing in the winter. A lady love might come up with ridiculous and over-the-top needs for attention. These were called exaggerated affectations; this is the specialty of the Red-hot Lover Drama King/Queen. It's all in the interests of maintaining the attention of others on his/her every thought and feeling. This is his/her passion and pride; his/her worst fate is feeling invisible.

Although there are people who complain about Red-hot Lovers and criticize them, there are just as many who adore them and wouldn't change them for anything in the world. After all, Red-hot Lovers are the people who are capable of going to any lengths for love. Just like any true knight errant in search of the prince/princess of his/her dreams, he/she is empowered by love; sometimes it feels like he/she is love itself. But the most enduring impact of the courtly lovers is on the hearts of lovers who passed down a sensitivity and openness to passion. They created a high value on passion-based love that shows up in all the world's great love stories. The Red-hot Lover has honorable, royal roots and holds a powerful place in everyone's concept of love.

www.ingramcontent.com/pod-product-compliance
Lightning Source LLC
Chambersburg PA
CBHW061341040426
42444CB00011B/3023